A Woolly Mammoth Journey

by **Debbie S. Miller** ❖ Pictures by **Jon Van Zyle**

Little, Brown and Company
Boston New York London

For the Caulfield family

Rick, Annie, Caitlin, Michael, and Julia

YOU HAVE JOURNEYED FAR.

THANKS FOR YOUR FRIENDSHIP, LOVE OF BOOKS,

AND SUPPORT OVER THE YEARS.

A special thanks to Adrian Lister for his research, thoughtful critique, and his wonderful book, *Mammoths*. Many thanks to Dale Guthrie, Paul Matheus, and Richard Nelson for reviewing the manuscript and answering questions. I'm grateful to Roland Gangloff and Glen Storrs for showing me bone and fossil collections at the University of Alaska Museum and the Natural History Museum in Cincinnati. Thanks to Cyndi Rybachek's family and Hardy Smith for sharing their discovery story and to Cynthia Moss, whose book *Elephant Memories* introduced me to the fascinating lives of African elephants. Last, thanks to the Fairbanks SCBWI writers' group, editor Laura Marsh, and my family, who drifted with me into the last Ice Age.

First Edition

Library of Congress Cataloging-in-Publication Data

Miller, Debbie S.
A woolly mammoth journey / by Debbie S. Miller ; illustrated by Jon Van Zyle. –1st. ed.
p. cm.
Summary: A great woolly mammoth leads her family across rivers, plains, and glacial ridges on an annual migration to familiar feeding grounds during a journey which happened more than 12,000 years ago.
ISBN 0-316-57212-8
1. Woolly mammoth – Juvenile literature. [1. Woolly mammoth. 2. Mammoths. 3. Prehistoric animals.] I. Van Zyle, Jon, ill. II. Title.
QE882.P8 M55 2001
569'.67– dc21 99-042428

10 9 8 7 6 5 4 3 2 1

TWP

Printed in Singapore

The paintings in this book were done in acrylic on untempered Masonite panels. The text was set in Popple-Pontifex and the display type is WoolyBully.

One summer day in 1978, ten-year-old Cyndi Rybachek discovered a giant tusk of a woolly mammoth along a tributary of the Tanana River near Fairbanks, Alaska. Turning back the clock, this story describes how that mammoth and its family might have lived 10,000 to 12,000 years ago, near the end of the last Ice Age.

As winds lash the top of the world, a family of woolly mammoths travels across the treeless, windswept plain known as the Mammoth Steppe. From a distance these shaggy cousins of the elephant look like walking haystacks. Long skirts of fur ripple in the wind, and dense coats of underwool insulate these enormous six-ton creatures.

Facing the wind, with trunks swaying, the mammoths follow Wise One. This fifty-year-old female is the oldest member and matriarch of the family. For many years, she has guided them along familiar trails, across deep rivers, and over ridges fringed with glaciers.

Wise One probes the stubbled ground for the first green grass that her family has long awaited. With spring days growing warmer, a few green shoots have begun to appear. Wise One's two-fingered trunk breaks off a clump of grass and stuffs it into her mouth. After months of grinding stubble and twigs between her foot-long molars, she welcomes the taste of fresh grass.

Wise One has given birth to seven calves in her life. Three of them perished during their first year because of long, severe winters. Now she lives with her two adult daughters, a ten-year-old son, and several grandsons and granddaughters. The youngest calf, a playful two-year-old, is her only great-grandson.

While the family grazes, Playful One chases Small Tusks, a four-year-old calf. They bump into their aunts and uncles, running in circles around them. After a good game of tag, Small Tusks tires and lies on his side while Playful One climbs and rolls over him. Playful One has boundless energy.

Wise One's youngest daughter grows restless while the bull calves tumble and roll. She shifts her weight from side to side and softly rumbles. Soon she will give birth to her first calf after a pregnancy that has lasted nearly two years.

After several hours, the wet face of a 200-pound female calf emerges from the mother mammoth. The female mammoths assist the mother like midwives. They pull the fetal sac away from Little One, greet her with stroking trunks, and lift her with their feet and tusks. Within a few minutes, Little One takes her first wobbly steps toward her mother.

During the first few days, Little One stays at her mother's side, learning how to suckle her rich milk. She curiously sniffs and probes the new world around her. All of the mammoths visit the calf, touching her with their trunks and welcoming her as the tenth family member. Playful One enjoys the idea of a new playmate. He greets Little One with a bold shove, nearly knocking her off her feet. The new mother gently pushes Playful One away and grunts at him.

The wind allows a pair of lions to pick up the distant scent of the newborn's fetal sac. Crouched low, they stalk the mammoth family on silent paws. The lions spot the new calf and move closer. Wise One lifts her trunk, cautiously sniffing the air. She is the first to smell danger. The lions close in. Immediately she reacts with a rumbling alarm call, warning the family that predators are near. The adults form a semicircle beside Wise One, with the young calves protected behind them.

One of the lions bolts forward, hoping that he can take the smallest calf by surprise. He bursts to a speed of thirty miles per hour, but Wise One sees him. She bows her head and charges the lion with sharp tusks lowered. The lion turns sharply and retreats to his mate. Although the 500-pound lion is one of the largest carnivores on earth, he is no match for a mammoth that weighs at least twelve times more. The lions head off in search of bison and other smaller prey.

One of the lions bolts forward, hoping that he can take the smallest calf by surprise. He bursts to a speed of thirty miles per hour, but Wise One sees him. She bows her head and charges the lion with sharp tusks lowered. The lion turns sharply and retreats to his mate. Although the 500-pound lion is one of the largest carnivores on earth, he is no match for a mammoth that weighs at least twelve times more. The lions head off in search of bison and other smaller prey.

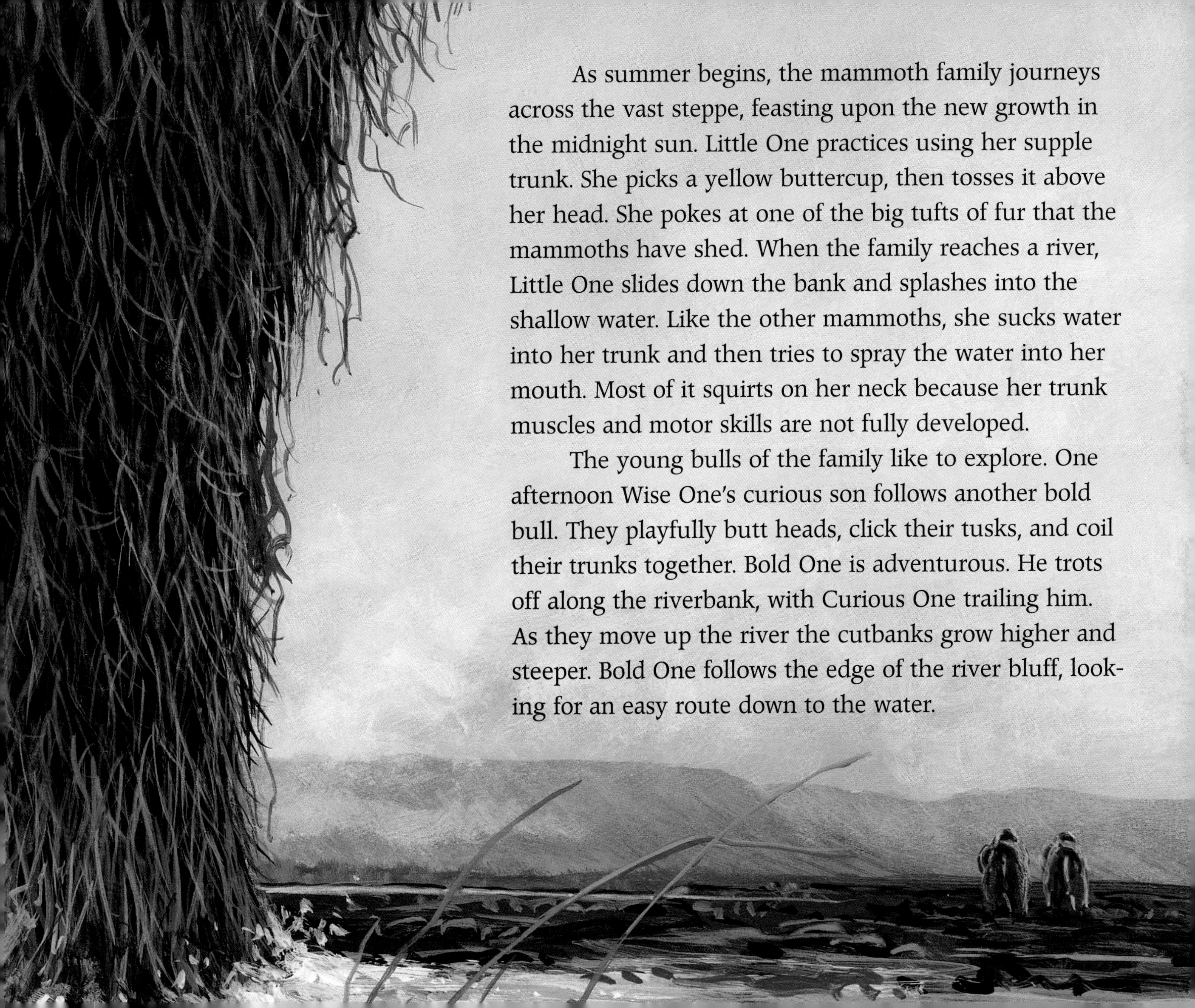

As summer begins, the mammoth family journeys across the vast steppe, feasting upon the new growth in the midnight sun. Little One practices using her supple trunk. She picks a yellow buttercup, then tosses it above her head. She pokes at one of the big tufts of fur that the mammoths have shed. When the family reaches a river, Little One slides down the bank and splashes into the shallow water. Like the other mammoths, she sucks water into her trunk and then tries to spray the water into her mouth. Most of it squirts on her neck because her trunk muscles and motor skills are not fully developed.

The young bulls of the family like to explore. One afternoon Wise One's curious son follows another bold bull. They playfully butt heads, click their tusks, and coil their trunks together. Bold One is adventurous. He trots off along the riverbank, with Curious One trailing him. As they move up the river the cutbanks grow higher and steeper. Bold One follows the edge of the river bluff, looking for an easy route down to the water.

Suddenly, a huge wedge of ground collapses beneath Bold One. He tumbles down the steep slope in a landslide of dirt and boulders. Curious One can no longer see Bold One and trumpets loudly in fright.

Wise One hears her son's cries echo across the valley. As she runs up the river, a cloud of dust rises above the landslide. Wise One finds her anxious son and leads him to the base of the bluff where Bold One fell. They find him partially buried in dirt and rocks. Wise One strokes the bull with her trunk and attempts to lift his body with her feet and tusks, but it is hopeless. The steep fall has severed the bull's spinal cord, killing him quickly.

For years to come, Wise One's family and their many relatives will not forget Bold One. Along this river the mammoths will pause and take time to visit the skeletal remains. The trunks of many mammoths will stroke the bones and tusks of the young bull, as though his spirit is always present.

One afternoon, huge cumulus clouds drift above the steppe, casting dark shadows on the mammoths. Wise One sniffs the air and smells rain. As temperatures cool it is a good time to move the family to a new feeding area. Wise One leads the group along a familiar old trail toward a distant river.

The rain is refreshing as they migrate for many miles. Along their journey they pass other groups of herbivores: bison and horses, musk oxen and caribou, saiga antelope and camels. Wise One is always wary of predators, such as saber-toothed cats, short-faced bears, or lions that might be lurking in the brush. Little One trots to keep up with the family. When she tires, her mother stops to let her rest and suckle. She drinks several gallons of milk each day and grows quickly.

At last the mammoths arrive at the big muddy river that they must cross to reach their favorite feeding area. They step into the glacial, silted water. Wise One and her daughter wade with Little One between them. To breathe, the mammoths hold their snorkel-like trunks above the water. As they cross the deepest part of the river, Wise One acts as a breaker against the strong current, protecting Little One from being washed away.

The family reaches the other side of the river and the mammoths shake the water out of their fur. Wise One raises her trunk to test the wind. She smells a new, strange scent. In the willow thickets above the river, people are roasting bison meat over a fire. Newcomers to the area, these nomadic hunters will live along this waterway for thousands of years to come.

As they approach their summer feeding area, Wise One hears a distant, familiar rumble. It is another family of mammoths. Wise One announces their arrival with a loud trumpet. The family responds with bellows and trumpets. The younger mammoths are excited and trot toward the group with trunks swinging and ears flapping.

Wise One recognizes the matriarch of the family. She is a cousin, whom Wise One has not seen in a year. They greet each other with friendly rumbles, clicking of tusks, and intertwined trunks. Playful One and Small Tusks run off to play with the young bulls. Little One discovers another calf close to her age. The gathering of the two families is a joyous celebration.

One morning a large bull mammoth joins Wise One's family. He is in musth (pronounced "must"), seeking a mate. Tears stream from his temporal glands and he gives off a strong odor. The bull is in prime condition and has long, curving tusks. A younger bull challenges Long Tusks for Wise One's youngest granddaughter. *Clack!* The two bulls charge each other, butting heads and whacking tusks together. The young bull soon realizes that he is no match for Long Tusks. He runs off, while Long Tusks lopes after the granddaughter. In two years' time, Playful One will have a new cousin.

As the summer days grow shorter, the families graze constantly to build up their fat reserves for the long winter. Each animal eats an average of 400 pounds of grasses and plants per day. Little One still suckles her mother, but she also pulls up small bunches of grass. As she chews, her gums swell. Her six-month molars are beginning to erupt, as well as her first set of milk tusks.

The family is preparing for the winter. They will each gain a thick layer of fat to fuel them during the coldest months. Their dense underwool and long guard hairs will insulate them. Fat deposits near their bulging heads and huge shoulders will also serve as emergency fuel. When necessary, their heavy tusks will crack through ice and dig through snow to reach food and water. These adaptations will enable them to survive the coming winter.

Night skies return, temperatures drop, and the wind blows steadily. The two mammoth families separate and move to hilly areas that are sheltered from the winter gales. As Wise One leads her family across the steppe, the first winter snowflakes dust the fur coats of the mammoths.

When the mammoths reach their winter range, the sky clears and the wind is less fierce. Little One is tired and hungry. She nudges one of her mother's front legs and begins suckling as night falls. After a few minutes, Little One pauses to listen to a new sound. Wolves howl on the nearby ridge in the face of a rising, brilliant moon.

One by one, the mammoths lie down to rest. First, Little One lies down and listens to the singing wolves. Then Small Tusks and Playful One lie beside her. The older animals join them. Always watchful, Wise One is the last to settle down for the night. In the coming months, she will lead and protect her family through the harsh winter, with dreams of spring.

Unlike dinosaurs, which became extinct about 65 million years ago, mammoths and other Ice Age mammals lived on earth during more recent times. Well-adapted to cold climates, woolly mammoths lived during the Pleistocene period, some 10,000 to 250,000 years ago. They gradually moved eastward from Europe and Siberia into Alaska across a land area known as Beringia, which once bridged North America and Asia. This story is set in interior Alaska, where many mammoth tusks and bones have been discovered.

The word *mammoth* is believed to be of Estonian origin. *Maa* means earth and *mutt* means mole. People once thought mammoths were gigantic moles that lived underground and died when exposed to light, because mammoth remains were often discovered partially buried.

HEIGHT: 9–11 feet tall
WEIGHT:
males: up to 6 tons, about the same size as an adult African elephant
females: 3–4 tons
calves: about 200 pounds at birth

PHYSICAL DESCRIPTION:
body: sloping back, dome-shaped head, small ears, short tail
fur: shaggy guard hairs up to 3 feet long and a dense layer of underwool
skin: about 1 inch thick with a 3–4 inch layer of fat beneath
teeth: huge brick-shaped molars, 1 foot or longer, 4 pounds in weight
trunk: about 6 feet long with 2 fingerlike projections at tip
temporal glands: glands near the temples that secrete tears with a distinct scent that may have signaled other animals
TUSKS: curved and twisted, average growth 1–6 inches per year
males: 8–9 feet long, average tusk weight 100 pounds
females: 5–6 feet long, average tusk weight 20–25 pounds
calves: At 6 months of age, milk tusks erupted. These tiny, 1–2 inch temporary tusks were replaced by permanent tusks after the calf's first year.

RANGE AND HABITAT: Woolly mammoths had a vast range stretching from Europe, through Siberia and Alaska, and south across Canada into the northernmost regions of the United States. They lived on an open, grassy plain known as the Mammoth Steppe.

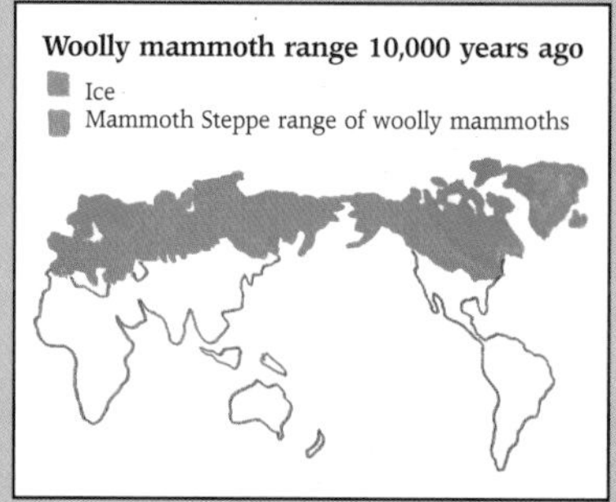

Adapted from *Mammoths* by Adrian Lister and Paul Bahn, Prentice Hall & IBD, 1994.

diet: about 400 pounds of grasses and plants per day.
predators: lions, saber-toothed and scimitar-toothed cats, short-faced bears, the spotted hyena in Europe, and in some parts of the world, humans
relatives: Mammoths were not direct ancestors of today's African and Asian elephants, but they are believed to be close cousins. Their physical characteristics, life cycle, and behavior were similar to those of our modern elephants.

LIFE SPAN: believed to be about 60 years

RECENT DISCOVERY: In 1997 an adult male mammoth was found in Siberia by a 9-year-old boy. Two years later, the entire body of the mammoth was excavated from an ice field to be studied by an international team of scientists. The freezing temperatures preserved the mammoth's body so well that the hair, skin, and even stomach contents can reveal information about the mammoth's life long ago.

NOTE ABOUT EXTINCTION: About 10,000 years ago mammoths had completely disappeared, except for one population of smaller animals on Wrangel Island, north of Siberia. (These lived as recently as 3,700 years ago.) What caused the mammoths and other Ice Age mammals to die out? One theory suggests that a dramatic change in climate may have caused the extinction. Another theory points to an increase in human population and hunting. One thing is certain: Many species of large mammals on several continents died out near the end of the last Ice Age. Through fossils, skeletons, and scientific research, we can discover how these animals lived and imagine them in our backyards thousands of years ago.